TAROT CARDS

The Ultimate Guide to Tarot Reading

(An Essential Beginner's Guide to Psychic Tarot Reading and Tarot Card Meanings)

Loretta Johnson

Published by Sharon Lohan

© **Loretta Johnson**

All Rights Reserved

Tarot Cards: The Ultimate Guide to Tarot Reading (An Essential Beginner's Guide to Psychic Tarot Reading and Tarot Card Meanings)

ISBN 978-1-990334-69-6

All rights reserved. No part of this guide may be reproduced in any form without permission in writing from the publisher except in the case of brief quotations embodied in critical articles or reviews.

Legal & Disclaimer

The information contained in this book is not designed to replace or take the place of any form of medicine or professional medical advice. The information in this book has been provided for educational and entertainment purposes only.

The information contained in this book has been compiled from sources deemed reliable, and it is accurate to the best of the Author's knowledge; however, the Author cannot guarantee its accuracy and validity and cannot be held liable for any errors or omissions. Changes are periodically made to this book. You must consult your doctor or get professional medical advice before using any of the suggested remedies, techniques, or information in this book.

Upon using the information contained in this book, you agree to hold harmless the Author from and against any damages, costs, and expenses, including any legal fees potentially resulting from the application of any of the information provided by this guide. This disclaimer applies to any damages or injury caused by the use and application, whether directly or indirectly, of any advice or information presented, whether for breach of contract, tort, negligence, personal injury, criminal intent, or under any other cause of action.

You agree to accept all risks of using the information presented inside this book. You need to consult a professional medical practitioner in order to ensure you are both able and healthy enough to participate in this program.

Table of Contents

INTRODUCTION 1

CHAPTER1: WHAT ARE TAROT CARDS? 2

CHAPTER 2: TAROT SPREADS 8

CHAPTER 3: SPREADING THE CARDS 19

CHAPTER 4: HOW TO LOOK AFTER YOUR DECK? 28

CHAPTER 5: BASIC DECK TYPES 40

CHAPTER 6: UNDERSTANDING THE MAJOR AND MINOR ARCANA 49

CHAPTER 7: HISTORY OF THE SYMBOLISM OF THE TAROT: INQÜIRY INTO ITS ORIGIN 58

CHAPTER 8: SWORDS 71

CHAPTER 9: TAROT CARDS READING AND PSYCHIC READING 87

CHAPTER 10: WAITE TAROT - INFORMATION ABOUT WAITE TAROT 116

CONCLUSION 135

Introduction

Did you already perform tarot and now you're wondering if there's more?

Have you tired of the same old spreads and you'd like something different?

Maybe you'd even like to create your own spread?

Well, you'll find all that information and a lot more in this advanced guide to tarot reading! You'll find spreads for many different questions, how to create your own spread, and the meanings for the cups, swords, wands, and pentacle suits; otherwise known as the minor arcana.

Read on to learn more!

Chapter1: What Are Tarot Cards?

At the first mention of tarot cards, a lot of stereotypical thoughts have already crossed you mind. Something like fortune telling, a woman with long robs shrouded in mystery and the thought of knowing a person's life and death. This is actually what popular culture has lead us to believe. There are tons of shows where a character would get his or her fortune told and tarot cards would always be present. Next thing that happens is that they pick a card and voila! They grab a card meaning death and after a few minutes in the character actually dies. It's a quite common and predictable scene actually.

But, what really are tarot cards? These set of cards are one of the most misunderstood cards ever. Quite frankly, tarot cards are just a set of playing cards. Yes, you read right and it's still being played in a lot of countries in Europe. Basically as a player, you must trump if you're left with no cards and tarot games are usually point-trick games. Each card has a value which depends on the game.

A tarot deck normally has about 78 playing cards which have some similarities if you compare them to a normal deck of playing cards. Tarot cards have four suits, but it still does vary and depend on the region. Each of the said suit contains pip cards that are numbered from one or ace, all the way to 10. Also there are four face cards namely the King, Queen, Knight and the Jack or Knave. So that's 14 cards in total.

Also, tarot cards has a separate 21-card trump suit, in addition there's also a card called the Fool. Just like the joker, its use depends on the game being played. It's either the trump card or some card that you won't include in the game. Initially, the game played using the tarot cards was called triumph and it's very similar to the modern game bridge.

Way back when tarot cards were still being developed, wealthy Italian families would hire and pay professional artists to make decks for them. The decks were known as "carte da trionfi" or "cards of triumph." At first the cards were marked with coins, polo sticks, swords and etc. The only members of the court back then were the king and two male underlings. It was only later that queens, triumphs and the fool was added to the deck.

Over-time, this card set has been associated with numerous beliefs; namely the supernatural, divinatory, esoteric and more. At first glance, a person that has no idea about the cards may find them a little bit intimidating and weird. It can be so mysterious to other people, because the belief that each of these cards possess are shaped by the era they were in; since tarot cards have been present for centuries. Take note, these cards might be the most famous ones when fortune telling is involved, but there are other tools too like the ordinary playing cards and the oracle decks.

Another thing that has greatly contributed to this deck being misunderstood is the way they were designed. A lot of the cards depict everyday life and circumstances that people experience every day. Originally, it was to depict the average life of the player way back then. Until, as time passed, it took in more and more meaning that's quite far-fetched from the initial intent; it was for gaming purposes only.

But where exactly did tarot cards come from? And who invented them? Well, it is believed that traditional playing cards came into view before the tarot cards. Common playing cards were already seen in Europe way back in 1375, it was introduced by Islamic societies. Take note that the Islamic societies have been using it long before they introduced it in Europe. Though there is no report or record that tarot cards were also present during that time. So there's no evidence that support the belief that the common playing cards were designed after tarot cards.

Tarot cards were believed to be first mentioned by the Duke of Milan in one of his letter way back in 1440. He wanted a couple of "triumph" cards that were supposed to be used in a certain event. The Duke differentiated the common playing cards from the triumph cards that he requested. When the game was introduced, it spread like wild fire all over Europe and in 1530 it was called tarocchi. The word tarocchi was the Italian form of the word tarot, which is French.

Then in 1781, the tarot cards were discovered by occult followers in England and France. As we said, the graphic were surreal and enchanting, which gained the attention of the occults. They thought that the cards held a much deeper meaning and are more than just simple playing cards. So they used tarot cards as their divination tools, they even wrote about it and it was entitled "the Tarot." One thing lead to another until the tarot cards became a permanent part of occult philosophy.

There is also the other belief where the tarot cards came all the way from Egypt. Also, there are those few that believe the tarot cards were the only "book" that survived from the great fire, the fire that destroyed the libraries of ancient Egypt. Taking that belief into account, tarot cards were considered as hieroglyphical keys to life.

The mythical beliefs associated with tarot cards alongside the theories concerning Egypt has spread all over Europe by mid-18th century. According to French writer Antoine Court de Gébelin, tarot cards were made from holy books that were written by Egyptian priests. He also stated that Gypsies from Africa introduced it in Europe. Which was highly unlikely since tarot cards actually came to the scene before Gypsies got to Europe. Not only that, but since the gypsies came from Asia and not Africa. But his words and his book had a major influence back then.

Chapter 2: Tarot Spreads

A tarot spread is simply the way the cards are laid out on the table. There are many different tarot spreads and the difference is how the cards are laid out.

The first spread I want to look at is a very basic tarot spread and it is called the Celtic cross. You will lay the first card down on the table, card two is place on top of card one turned sideways and placed near the bottom of card one. Card 3 is placed directly below card one, 4 is placed to the left of card one, 5 is placed above card one, 6 is placed to the right of card 1.

Now you will move slightly to the right of card 6, place card 7 down on the table, 8 will be placed above 7, 9 above 8, and 10 above 9.

This spread is usually used for a general reading although it can be used for a question based reading. Now you will need to understand how the position of the cards affect each card in this spread.

In the Celtic spread:

Card 1 describes what is currently influences the one who is seeking answers.

Card 2 describes the obstacles that are blocking the person who is seeking answers.

Card 3 describes something that has recently happened in the past that had a direct influence on the current situation.

Card 4 describes the past situations that the seeker has had to deal with.

Card 5 describes what the seeker is wishing to achieve.

Card 6 describes what the future of the seeker will hold if they continue on the path they are currently following.

Card 7 is used to learn about the seekers attitude toward their current situation.

Card 8 describes how others see the seeker.

Card 9 helps the seeker learn about their hopes and fears.

Card 10 describes the final outcome of the situation if the person continues following the path they are currently following.

Now I want to make it clear that when I say if the person continues to follow the current path they are on, it means that just because a tarot reading says something is going to happen does not mean these events are set in stone. You should talk to the person about different courses they could take in order to avoid negative outcomes in specific situations of their lives.

This is usually the spread that most people begin using because it is a basic tarot spread, it is also very easy to understand as well as remember what the different positions mean about each card.

Next is the five card spread. You will lay card one down on the table this will become the center of the spread. The other 4 cards will be laid around card one. Card 2 will be laid just to the left of card one, card 3 will be laid to the right of card one, card 4 will be laid just below card one, and card 5 will be laid just above card one.

This is another very simple spread and in order for it to work you need to know what each position means.

The card one position in this spread represents the current situation or the area of the seekers life in which all of the other cards will revolve around.

The card two position in this spread represents the past influences in the seekers life that are still having an effect on their life. It usually represents something in the persons past that is having a direct effect on the situation that is represented by card one.

The card three position in this spread represents the future of the seeker in the situation represented by card one if the seeker continues on their current path.

The card four positon in this spread represents the reason the seeker asked the specific question and it will usually shed some light on the meaning of card two.

The card five position in this spread represents what is possible in the situation. It does not give a definite outcome or does not predict the future but instead can give either a positive outcome if the seeker changes the path they are currently on or a negative outcome if the seeker continues on the same path and vice versa.

This spread is very useful when a person is seeking a specific direction in a specific area of their life.

The next spread is the ellipse spread. This spread contains seven cards and is in the shape of a V. Card one being the top of the V followed by 2 and 3, 4 being the point of the V followed by 5 and 6 with 7 finishing up the other side of the V.

Card one of this spread is going to describe how the past is affecting the current situation.

Card two of this spread is going to describe what is currently going on in your life that is affecting the situation the seeker is wanting answers about.

Card three of this spread is going to describe what future influences will come in to play in the specific situation.

Card four of this spread is going to explain what the seeker should do in the current situation.

Card five of this spread is going to explain any external influences that have bearing on the current situation.

Card six of this spread will discuss the hopes and fears of the seeker.

Card seven of this spread will discuss the final outcome of the situation if the seeker continues on the current path they are following.

The fourth spread I want to teach you is the relationship spread. This spread contains 10 cards and is laid out as follows:

Card 1 is laid on the table followed by 2, 3, 4 and 5 creating a row of cards. Card 6 is placed above card 3 card 7 is placed below cards 3 and 4, card 8 is placed below cards 2 and 4. Card 9 is placed above card 6 with card 10 to the right of card 9.

Now that you have the cards laid out you need to understand what each of the positions signifies.

Card ones position in this spread will describe the distant past concerning relationships.

Card twos position in this spread will describe the recent past concerning the relationships of the seeker.

Card threes position in this spread will describe the current situation.

Card fours position in this spread will describe the external influences that concern the seekers relationships.

Card fives position in this spread will describe the seekers attitude toward relationships.

Card sixes position in this spread will describe any helpful energies that can be used by the seeker.

Card sevens position in this spread will describe all future influences.

Card eights position in this spread will discuss any obstacles the seeker needs to overcome.

Card nines position in this spread will discuss the seekers hopes and fears.

Card tens position in this spread will discuss the final result if the seeker continues on the current path they are following.

The final spread I want to teach you in this chapter is the mirror spread. This spread contains 8 cards and is laid out as follows:

Card one is laid at the top of the spread. The rest of the cards will be laid below card one on either side of the card. Card two will go below and to the left of card one. Card three will go below and to the right of card one. Card four will go below card two, card five will go below card three, card six will go below card for and card seven will go below card five. The final card, card eight will go at the bottom of the spread in direct line with card one.

Now that you understand how to lay out this spread you can begin learning how the positions of each card affect their meaning.

The card one position in this spread represents the seeker.

The card two position in this spread represents the seeker sees the other people in the situation.

The card three position in this spread represents what the other people in the situation represent to the seeker.

The card four position in this spread represents the obstacles within the situation.

The card five position in this spread represents how the others in the situation view themselves.

The card six position in this spread describes what you represent to the others in the situation.

The card seven position in this spread describes the strengths within the situation.

The card eight position in this spread discusses the outcome of the situation if the seeker continues to follow the current path they are on.

There are hundreds of different spreads that can be used with tarot cards, some of them focusing on specific areas such as careers or love and some are general spreads. These that you have learned in this chapter are basic spreads that can be used when you are first learning about tarot cards all the way up until you are an expert and beyond.

I suggest that you start with the Celtic cross and once this spread is mastered you can move on to a different spread and learn it. Take your time as you are learning spreads. If it is helpful, draw the spreads in a notebook and jot down notes about what the different card positions represent.

Chapter 3: Spreading The Cards

After going through the meanings of the Major Arcana cards, you need to move forward to reading them. Here is what you need to do.

Relax

Practice deep breathing, drink cool water or do whatever that relaxes and calms your nerves. Being calm before reading the tarot is substantial to correctly interpreting the meanings of the cards you draw. When you're calm, your mind relaxes and this helps you listen to your intuitive voice easily. Try to let go of your worries for now, so you can focus completely on the reading. Also, ensure you are seated in a quiet area with minimum to no distractions, so you can ruminate on the meaning of the cards effortlessly.

Clear the deck

Next, you need to clear your deck of tarot cards of any sort of residual energy. This is the leftover energy from the last reading. Tarot cards absorb the energy from the person who touches or reads them. Therefore, if anyone touched your cards or read them, you need to clear them of the residual energy before reading them again. The most effective way of doing this is via shuffling your cards. Shuffle the deck a couple of times. Then, you need to visualize that you are standing in a shining white light and are breathing it. Imagine absorbing that energy in your arms and hands, and then sending it to your tarot cards, so they bathe in that beautiful light too. This is an excellent way of clearing your cards of any leftover energy and helping you connect strongly to them.

Ask a question

After clearing the deck of any residual energy, you need to silently ask any question you want answers to in your mind. You can also ask it aloud as well. If you are reading someone, ask him or her to speak their question out loud. In case, there isn't any specific question in your mind at the moment, you can simply ask the cards 'What message do you want to give me today?' or 'Is there something I need to be aware of now?' Next, you need to enable your question slowly settle in the deck and envision that it is traveling to the deck from your mind.

Spreading the cards

You need to shuffle your cards again and keep shuffling them until you get the feeling that you need to stop. Now, you have to cut your deck using your left hand. Mostly, tarot card readers cut the deck by dividing it into three piles. After doing that, you should ask the person you are reading to pick a pile from which you can draw the cards. If you are reading your own self, then you should select a pile that you feel connected to. You can also cut it in half, placing the topmost half on your left side. There are different sorts of spreads, but for beginners, it is best to stick to the two basic ones: three-card and Celtic cross spreads.

The 3-Card Spread

This spread works well for yes or no questions. After cutting your deck, you need to lay them moving from left to your right.

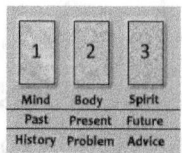

The first card represents your past, any issues that affected you in your past and issues pertinent to your mind. The second card signifies the present and issues related to your present. It also speaks about your body. The third card is pertinent to the spirit and helps you predict the future and outcomes of different matters. This spread is also known as the 'mind, body, and spirit' spread as it gives you a general understanding of how well you or the person you are reading is doing in these respective areas.

Celtic-Cross Spread

The Celtic-cross spread is one of the most commonly used and detailed spreads of tarot reading. It is good to use when you have a complicated question and you want to understand its answer in detail. This spread gives you a systematic view of the issue and helps you understand all the aspects related to your problem. To use it, you need to lay your cards in the order shown below.

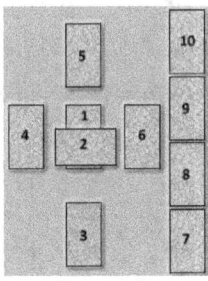

• The first card represents the 'querent' and signifies the person who has asked the question. Although, it points the person who has a query, it can at times signify someone in the querent's life- someone close to him or her, or someone who is related to the querent's issue.

• The second card represents the situation and issue at hand. It might not always be relevant to the question being asked, and might point to the question that should have been asked. This card signifies the solution for a problem, or the obstacles encountered by the querent.

• The third card shows the foundation. It helps understand the elements that have given rise to the querent's problem; they are usually issues from the past. It acts as the foundation on which the issue is built upon.

• The fourth card represents the querent's recent past. It is mostly linked to the third card. For instance, if the third card indicates financial crisis, the fourth card may show that the querent lost their sole job, which is why they are experiencing a financial issue. However, if the entire reading is a positive one, the fourth card might point towards happy incidents that have occurred recently.

• The fifth card is representative of the events and episodes that are quite likely to occur in the querent's near future, probably in the next couple of months. It displays the circumstances that are going to form and then unfold.

• The sixth card is indicative of the present situation being faced by the querent. It tells you whether the problem will be getting resolved soon or not. It shows where the querent stands in relation with the solution, or future outcome.

• The seventh card is representative of the outside influences. It tells you which people are supporting the querent and the people who would be affecting the expected or desired outcome.

• The eighth card signifies the internal influences. How is the querent feeling about their situation? This card will give you a true insight into the querent's feelings and will help you better understand the situation.

• The ninth card symbolizes the querent's hopes and fears. It is similar to the eighth card, but throws better lights on all the querent wants and everything that scares them.

• The tenth card represents the long-term outcomes. Mostly, it acts as the conclusion of all the nine cards. The querent will experience the outcome shown by this card in about six to seven months, or maybe a year at times. In case this card seems vague and you are not able to understand its meaning, you should pull out one or maybe two more tarot cards and put them in the exact position of the tenth card and join them with the other cards to comprehend its meaning.

You need to choose any of these two spreads, or any other if you prefer depending on your question or someone else's question if you are reading anybody else. Next, you need to move on to interpreting the cards, so you can interpret their meaning and comprehend what they are trying to tell you.

Chapter 4: How To Look After Your Deck?

For each individual, their tarot card deck is precious and valuable. It is not the material value of them that matters, it is what they mean to you personally. After all, each deck of cards is made of paper, and they are susceptible to wear and tear. There are two important things to take into consideration when you take care of them. First one is to keep them safe and clean and the second one is to charge them when they need it.

Tarot cards usually come in a wooden box, but these boxes are sometimes not durable enough. The more you use them, the more care they will need. Besides the box, some sets also come in a pouch. If your set did not come with a small pouch, you could buy one or even make one yourself if you have some basic sewing skills. You can use any material or your choice from velvet to satin or even from cotton. If you have kids or pets around, you will need to keep the cards away from their reach. Also, it is important to keep them in a dry place away from spills and sticky things. You can use a nonabrasive soft tissue to wipe them from time to time. Sometimes, we spill something on them. It is good to have a cleaning cloth handy for times like this.

The second most important thing is to charge the cards when they are "tired." Especially if you are reading for others. When others shuffle the cards, their energies reflect onto the cards. You may find after a few readings they do not make any sense, and your vision is clouded. There are two reasons for this: You are tired. You need to recharge your own batteries, or the cards need some time off. People prefer different methods when it comes to charging their cards. The most popular are to line them up in the original order, upright. Then gather them in that order and leave them in their pouch or box until you "feel" the time is right to reuse them. You can also charge them using sea salt. Spread your cards and sprinkle sea salt on them and wait for a while. Then collect them and dump the salt. Some people prefer the positive effects of the moonlight, either a full moon or a new moon. Since the moon has feminine energy and it represents the intuitive powers. Consider leaving your cards by your window at night where they will receive enough moonlight. Then put them back in their box until next time when you are ready to use them.

REMEMBER, if you see that you can not read a spread or if it is a total mumbo-jumbo, don't force it until recharged!

When you get familiar with the way the cards communicate with you, you will decide what is the best way for you to charge them. There is not one correct method. Each person will feel closer to one method over another.

RIDER-WAITE-SMITH DECK

A.E. Waite and Pamela Colman Smith created one of the world's most famous tarot deck. Waite made a living as a freelance author and translator. Smith was in performing arts. Both met when they become members of the Hermetic Order of the Golden Dawn. It was an organization formed in England. It brought together people interested in the occult, mysticism, and paranormal activities. Waite was aware of Smith's psychic abilities, and he paid her a flat fee to design the cards.

The deck consists of 78 cards: 22 major arcana and 56 minor arcana cards. The major arcana cards have a lot of similarities with Tarot de Marseille deck. Golden Dawn also influenced these cards and their symbols and meanings. The Rider-Waite-Smith deck follows a less Christian and a less Kabbalistic approach. Smith and Waite removed most of the religious symbols when they created the deck. Including the Jewish numbers. Instead, they followed a more occultist pattern. This was the right move as the deck became famous fast among tarot enthusiasts. The first deck saw the light of day in 1910.

To this day, this is the most popular set of all other decks due to it being easier to learn and understand. It is also the deck of choice for most of the beginners.

The most important thing that makes this deck unique for its time is its symbolism and imagery. Smith illustrated them all. This is the first time tarot enthusiasts saw a deck of cards that featured scenes and people. You can see people's faces, their reactions; you can see scenes that tell a story. You can see the numbers and colors corresponding to these scenes and the people on them. This was unheard of before Waite and Smith published their deck for the first time. Later, many people designed hundreds of sets with the influence from Rider-Waite-Smith symbolism. The pictures are for the most part quite simple to understand and to interpret. Each card tells its story. The cards draw you into their mystical, magical world in an instant. Smith captured lots of human emotions in this set. Which adds to the magic of the cards.

The images make it easier for an absolute beginner to remember the basic meanings of the cards. This is why it is one of the most important decks of all times. Also, most of the books that teach tarot will use this deck, so it is easier for anyone to access information on it. Once you master this set, you will find it much easier to move on to more occult sets without people and scenes on them. The symbols are so strong that you will find yourself drawn to their history without even realizing. This is also a good deck to start with for those who have an interest inWestern Esoteric traditions. Waite was involved in esoteric practices. When he commissioned Smith to give life to his ideas, he instructed her what he had in mind like occultism and mysticism.

TAROT DE MARSEILLE DECK

Tarot of Marseille influenced almost all the European tarot cards that came after it.

The deck originates from Northern Italy. The copy dates back to the 15th century. When tarot started losing popularity in Italy, the experts brought it to Southern France and Switzerland. In these places, tarot grabbed people's interest immediately and created a new wave. With this newfound popularity, the deck managed to go back to Italy, where it once again became popular. The name Tarot de Marseille is not as old as the deck itself. French occultist Papus named them as such in the late 19th century.

Like most of the decks, Tarot de Marseille has 56 cards that form the minor arcana. These are four standard suits as we know them. The deck has heavy Christian influences like the Pope, the Devil, the Grim Reaper. It also has nontraditional Christian images like the Papess. This card has created a lot of controversy among the practitioners of tarot. It shows a female pope. Many people believe that the card symbolizes Pope Joan. We do not have historical evidence about a female pope.

To avoid controversy, some decks used the names Juno, The Spanish Captain, and The High Priestess.

The 13th card of the deck as we refer to today as The Death had no name. The name La Mort (The Death) appears in the Tarot de Marseille much later. Because the deck included the Pope and Popess cards, the Catholic Church considered them as blasphemous. In certain areas, the Church demanded these cards to be replaced by other cards. Containing other images instead of religious ones. In certain decks, these characters became June and Jupiter. In other ones, they were The Spanish Captain and The Wine Barrel. The irony was that these characters were actually replaced by Pagan symbols. This was on purpose as a protest against the Church.

When Tarot de Marseille returned to Italy, two different styles became popular. These were Lombardy and Piemontese. In the beginning, the cards' designs were not much different than their French versions. They even had misspelled French titles.

Later, the cards took a different turn when they became double headed. The birthplace of the double-headed cards is Milan. This deck also has its unique design that is different than the original Tarot de Marseille.

This deck is still popular today. The single-headed design that is closer to the original design made a comeback. Tarot experts are more inspirational and more artistic. Cards from I to X have human figures. Cards from XI to XXII consist of more complex scenes and many people. Minor Arcana deal with more mundane situations. Major Arcana deal with deeper spiritual situations. Cards from 1 to 10 do not have any human figures; they only have the symbols of the suit they represent. King, Queen, Knight and Page have human figures. They represent the person they are symbolizing.

DIFFERENCES BETWEEN TAROT DE MARSEILLE AND RIDER-WAITE SMITH

The biggest difference between these two sets is their imagery. Rider-Waite-Smith minor arcana cards all have humans and scenes on them. Tarot de Marseille minor arcana cards only have humans for the court cards. The former has more modern graphics. Rider-Waite set has lesser religious symbols and more occult graphics. Because both Waite and Smith were into occultism.

Tarot de Marseille is still as popular as Rider-Waite-Smith deck. Rider-Waite-Smith is more popular in the Western Europe and Northern America. Especially in Northern America, there are hundreds of variations of this. It is also public domain. This enables artists to design their own versions of this set. However, in Western Europe, the set is not yet public domain and will remain so until 2022. Tarot de Marseille is the deck of choice for many Eastern Europeans still today. They are popular in non-English speaking countries.

Tarot de Marseille is also known as Latin Tarot. In the ancient times, these cards were popular as playing cards. That is why their designs have similarities with the traditional playing cards. The Justice card in the Tarot de Marseille is the 8th card, and the Strength card is number 11. The Death card used to have no name, the name La Mort appears in later versions. The Papess and The Pope in Latin Tarot became The High Priestess and The Hierophant in Rider-Waite-Smith deck. This is the biggest thing that makes them less religious.

Latin Tarot is more suitable for people who are more familiar with the symbols. Western cards are easier to interpret, and they are more suitable for beginners. Regardless, these differences do not make one or the other easier or more or less intuitive. Both sets have their strong imagery; this makes it easier for everyone to develop a personal connection. For the Latin Tarot, you will need a stronger memory to remember the meanings of particular cards because they do not include any scenes or humans. In the end, with more practice, this will not be a problem. Practice is the key for the tarot reading. The more you read, the easier it will get for you.

Chapter 5: Basic Deck Types

There is an amazing array of tarot decks to choose from, literally hundreds of them. Like any other tool that you will put to use, whether it is for hobbies, crafts, building a home or divination not every deck will work the same for the same person. Choosing a tarot deck is a personal process and you should expect it to take some trial and error. While there are hundreds of choices in decks there are some basic similarities. Every region has its own set up and how it assembles tarot decks. You can learn a lot about the region your deck was designed in by looking at the contents. In this chapter we will cover some of the basic varieties that can be found in tarot decks.

French suited decks

The French suited tarot decks appeared in Germany for the first time during the 18th century. That first generation of decks showed animal scenes on the trump cards causing the Germans to dub them

"Tiertarock" decks which literally mean animal cards. The current formation of French suited decks appears in this set of patterns:

Industrie und Glück:

Translated, this deck is called the Industry and the Luck deck. This style of deck uses Roman numerals on all of its triumphs and is standardly sold in a deck of 54 instead of 78. The 5 through 10 in red and the 1 through 6 of black have been removed.

Cego:

This deck first showed up in the Black Forest of Germany which shared a border with France and like the Industrie und Glück has 54 cards. Within this deck the cards have been organized like the Industrie und Glück but instead of using Roman numerals you will find Arabic numerals being used on the trumps, instead of being in the corners however these numbers are in the center.

Tarot Nouveu:

This deck is one of the most common varieties still in use in France today. It has 79 cards and the trumps use Arabic numerals placed within the corners.

The artwork that is done on each variety of French tarot cards is a sharp departure from that scene on the Italian designs which are older. The allegorical designs that were most common during the Renaissance were slowly abandoned to offer more whimsical themes that we see today. Many of these pictures showed scenes in daily life. One thing to note about the French tarot varieties is that even today they are still most commonly used for card games and not as commonly used for the purpose of divination. There are some cases, however, where the person set in the process of divination finds that a French styled deck is what speaks directly to them.

German suited decks

While it was the French decks that first made a showing in German it did not take long for them to adapt the decks and create their own regional variety. The German decks are very different then the French decks and most of them only have 36 cards in them. The cards that are most commonly included in the German decks are the numbers 6 through 10 the Under Knave, Over Knave, King and the Ace and there is no dedicated trump suit within the German tarot decks. German decks like French decks are not as commonly used for divination due to the small amount of cards in them, they are more commonly used to play a game called Schafkopf. Once again, however, choosing a deck willdepend on the user and while rarely some feel called to use a German deck.

Spanish suited decks

The Spanish generally use Italian styled decks, however there is the TaroccoSiciliano that is used regionally in Spain. It changes some of the trump cards within it and has a card specific to the deck called the destitution card. This deck also only has 64 cards instead of 78, the cards are also designed small and are not reversible.

Italian suited decks non-divination and divination

Now we come to the Italian suited tarot decks which are by all accounts the first decks created and the most commonly used among those who choose to do divination. There are decks set up for card games and specifically ones set up for divination. The decks used for divination get their origins, however, in the playing decks.

Tarocco Piemontese:

This deck has four suits within it coins, cups, batons and swords. Each one of the suits has the standard King and Queen then a caviler or knight and jack. You then get the pip cards and this deck totals 78 cards.

Swiss 1JJ Tarot:

Is very similar to the Tarocco deck, but it will replace the Pope and Popess cards with Jupiter and Juno. You also see the Angel replaced with Judgement and the Tower is called the house of god. Another key difference is that this deck is not reversible.

Tarocco Bolognese:

Is a deck of 62 cards many of the numeral cards are left out of this deck and offer different trumps then the other decks.

It was Etteilla who issued the first deck of tarot cards that were designed to be used specifically for divination. The first decks released for this purpose kept with the teachings of Thoth and themes that stayed in relation to the world of Ancient Egypt. Within a 78 card deck of cards specifically designed for divination there are two distinctive parts of the deck:

Major Arcana:

Also known as the greater secrets or as game players would call them trump cards have 22 cards with no suits. The cards are usually: The high priestess, the magician, the empress the emperor, the Hierophant, the lovers, the chariot, the world, the fool, the sun, the moon, judgement, the star, the tower, the devil, temperance, death, the hanged man, justice, wheel of fortune, the hermit and strength. All cards except the fool are given roman numerals, the fool has no number.

Minor Arcana:

Also known as the lesser secrets has 56 cards and they are –separated into four different suits with 14 cards in each suit. You get the court cards King, Queen, Knight and Page and then the ten numbered cards. You find the traditional Italian suits of swords, batons (also known as wands or staves or rods), coins (also known as dicks or pentacles) and cups being used in these decks.

The type of illustrations you can find within the divination decks is purely endless. From old style to modern style from widely colorful to simple black and white art. Along with these different artistic designs you will find different symbolism within each deck. This is why choosing ones tarot deck is a very personal thing that can take some time. With that said, some basic symbolism can be covered as many of the modern decks tend towards modifying traditional symbols that will reflect the beliefs of their creators.

Rider-Waite decks:

These decks move away from some of the traditional styles of tarot and uses scenery in the pip cards, it also gives rank to both the strength and justice cards.

Crowely-Harris deck of Thoth:

This is a very detailed deck and each card has an amazing amount of astrological, zodiacal, elemental and Qabalistic symbolism throughout. Even the colors used in these cards have symbolism of their own and are related to the elements, fire, water, air, earth and spirit. This set of tarot is not as common as the Rider-Waite decks, but has a deep spiritual meaning throughout.

Hermetic deck:

This set of tarot uses the imagery of the tarot and functions as a mnemonic device for teaching the gnosis of alchemical language and the philosophical meanings within. Most of these decks are black and white and stay with the simple artistic work.

What is listed here in this chapter is just the core basics of what you will find in decks of tarot. There are decks that come in all shapes and sizes, those aimed for cat lovers or those who relate to fire. Take your time when looking for a divination deck and find what speaks to you, so that when you start the process of readings you will get the best possible results.

Chapter 6: Understanding The Major And Minor Arcana

Each tarot perusing(reading) includes rearranging the Major and Minor Arcana cards, yet what's the distinction? Tarot utilizes images and pictures that invoke emotions to assist us with taking advantage of our own instinct. Understanding the distinction between the Major Arcana and Minor Arcana is basic, however luckily, it's likewise clear.

The cards are not structured only to show you the future, yet to assist you with understanding your view of the present so you can shape those discernments and alter your practices to produce the force you want throughout everyday life.

A Tarot perusing can decide whether we are gaining from our encounters or in the event that we are being overwhelmed by pessimism and neglecting to locate that silver coating. Since we live in a world made of importance dependent on reference to everything else on the planet, we as a whole have comparable encounters that we attribute certain unquestionable incentive to. Tarot perusing isn't intended to terrify us about the future at all and this is the place a few people totally misjudge how accommodating Tarot perusing really is.

For instance, when we split away from a harsh relationship, we are beginning another part and become progressively adroit at exploring future connections in view of the torment we experienced.

In the first place, how about we get a comprehension of the Major and Minor Arcana in a Tarot perusing request for you to open the intensity of the Tarot.

The Major Arcana in Tarot Reading

The Major Arcana pursues the development procedure that we experience by encountering life. We have hardships that enable us to learn and turn into a more astute rendition of ourselves. Tarot perusing can assist us with utilizing our background to develop by giving us a

10,000 foot perspective on our feelings and the cycles and impacts of our own behavior.

The cards in the Major Arcana help uncover our own propensities that can chomp us in the butt on the off chance that we don't get genuine with them. They can assist us with seeing in the event that we are on our overinflated ego or giving apprehension a chance to outwit us. The Major Arcana begins with the Fool card, who is an amateur who must experience the other 21 cards of the Major Arcana to get astute, somebody who can offer guidance to others when they get to the 22nd card, the World, which speaks to an individual adjusted in their capacity.

The Major Arcana encourages us tap into the most profound pieces of ourselves, for example, our instinct, inventiveness, authority, the intensity of our words, our capacity to choose when something isn't directly for us, and even the benefit of removing time to reflect. Since Tarot perusing spreads are set up to show us a course of events, we can even pick up knowledge into ways we were thinking in the past that have made our current circumstance and projection for what's to come.

Long story short, Major Arcana cards are about groundbreaking circumstances that shape our center convictions. They uncover when we are changing our objectives or when we are experiencing a transformation through our encounters. They enable us to advance to higher conditions of cognizance where we are engaged by our instinct by reflecting back to us our considerations that are helping or thwarting us so we can divert our bigger objectives and choices for our own more noteworthy great.

The Major Arcana uncovers when we are taking advantage of our female vitality and when we are drawing on our manly vitality. It causes us discover the intensity of our feelings(that has consistently been there!) so we can push our energies towards valuable goals. It additionally helps hint us into when we are depending a lot on rationale rather than profound direction, where we enable ourselves to be guided by spirits and to be bolstered by the inconspicuous messages of the soul domains and grandiose awareness.

There are extraordinary bits of knowledge offered from every one of the Major Arcana cards and they each have an interesting vitality from the photos and paradigms they speak to. Look at what every one of the Major Arcana cards intend to become more acquainted with them and start getting to your natural capacities.

The Minor Arcana in Tarot Reading

The littler activities and occasions that development to the significant snapshots of our life are portrayed through the Minor Arcana in your Tarot perusing. These activities are driven by considerations and convictions that are either useful or impeding. For instance, the little demonstration of eating a

McDonald's Upbeat Dinner consistently could be on the grounds that we are genuinely eating to muffle some agony we have to manage over.

The Minor Arcana cards show us the everyday encounters we will experience and assist us with understanding which parts of our brain are prevailing in specific circumstances. The 4 divisions of the 56 cards of the Minor Arcana speak to our cash (pentacles), our feelings (cups), our musings and words (swords), and our interests (wands).

Every one of these 4 classifications is numbered 1 through 10, which makes it simple to utilize the Minor Arcana for uncovering the subtleties of your own mind's inward activities. The even numbers 2, 4, 6, 8, and 10 speak to amicable vitality and things happening as expected. 1 is a fresh start, and 10 is the summit of a littler cycle in your life.

Every one of the 4 suits of the Minor Arcana likewise have 4 court cards, which are the page, the knight, the sovereign, and the lord. The page implies you're a beginner in some territory, simply beginning. The knight shows you're creating quality in a territory. The sovereign shows maternal characteristics, for example, sympathy and imagination, while the ruler shows a greater amount of your grounded, down to earth side

End

The Major Arcana cards are extraordinary at helping you pinpoint minutes throughout your life that molded your personality. They likewise assist you with seeing significant patterns that drive your way of life and can mean the distinction between getting hitched or not, having children or not, or changing occupations or not. The Minor Arcana cards help you know when your reasoning is dread based, when your feelings are outwitting you, or when littler triumphs are not too far off. Both the Major and Minor Arcana are significant and accommodating.

A few people are apprehensive when they see the cards, for example, the Fiend, Demise or the Pinnacle, and go into a frenzy that something terrible will occur. These cards are not intended to produce dread yet are really useful apparatuses. The Fiend card speaks to a dependence you may have, regardless of whether it is to an idea design or an individual who is affecting you negatively. Tarot perusing is intended to enable you to see your general surroundings and your part in it all the more unmistakably so you can secure yourself and settle on better choices with a progressively careful information on yourself. Likewise, the Passing card generally doesn't mean an exacting demise, however relinquishing a mental piece of yourself you never again need as your soul refines.

With both, it's critical to remember that what's to come isn't written in stone. A few people fear Tarot perusing since they think it uncovers a future that they can't take care of. Actually, Tarot readings just uncover designs that you can use to make energy to enable you to choose on the off chance that you need to proceed on a way or change course.

Chapter 7: History Of The Symbolism Of The Tarot: Inqüiry Into Its Origin

Beginning of the Symbolism of the Tarot as we have just expressed, each card of the Tarot speaks to an image, a number, and a thought. We have attempted to stay away from induction to the extent conceivable over the span of these clarifications and consequently we previously considered the numbers, for they are the most settled component and give the most unvarying outcomes in their blends. Depending solidly upon the premise which we have consequently developed, we would now be able to think about the images with supreme affirmation.

We trust that for this reason, you have obtained the Tarot of Marseilles, the most right in its imagery 1 or else the twenty-two cards planned by Oswald Wirth; Maybe—and this is actually practically crucial you have verified them two. You need, at that point, just arrangement the cards upon the table, to see on the double that the personages portrayed upon them upset wear dresses of the Renaissance period.1

But, is this pack of cards of antiquated cause? It doesn't show up so. Take a gander at your figures all the more mindfully and you will before long see Egyptian images [the triple cross (No. 5), and the ibis (No. 17)] joined with these Renaissance outfits. They without a moment's delay demonstrate that the Tarot of Marseilles is extremely the definitive portrayal of the crude Egyptian Tarot, marginally changed to the age indicated by the ensembles. Just the wanderers have the crude pack flawless.

The investigations of those showed men who have researched the Tarot have affirmed this reality by the most grounded proof. Furthermore, crafted by Chatto, 2 Boiteau, 3 or more all of Merlin, 4 give us that history supports our attestation. Merlin directed his inquires about deductively, furthermore, prevailing with regards to finding the first of our Tarot of Marseilles in an Italian Tarot at Venice, the dad of upset the later packs. He accepted likewise that he had found the starting point of this Venetian Tarot in the philosophical pack of Mantegna.

In any case, he couldn't decide the birthplace of this pack, since the one that Merlin accepted to be the source of the Tarot is, despite what might be expected, a proliferation, made by one of the Initiates. The Ars Magna of Raymond Lully was delivered similarly; it is drawn completely from the Tarot. We have given for reference the pack of Mantegna, referred to in the exchange as the cards of Balding, just as the packs of the Italian

Tarots, from which the greater part of our own are inferred.

Table 1 demonstrates the association between the Tarot packs and the arrangement of Mantegna should be turned around, and despite what might be expected show the cards of Mantegna gotten from the Tarot, as we have expressed. Here pursue the subtleties of different Tarot sets. Assuming, be that as it may, the presence of Egyptian images in these purported Italian Tarots doesn't persuade the pursuer, a couple of words on the change of the Tarot in the East, and in different nations of Europe other than Italy will totally illuminate him regarding the matter.

HINDU TAROTS

Fig. 29. Kaumbri

Notwithstanding Merlin's declarations, the Tarot speaks to the synopsis of the logical information on the people of yore. This is certainly demonstrated by Chatto s inquires about Orientalists regarding this matter.

Truth be told, the Indians have a round of chess, the Tchaturcmga, clearly got from the Tarot, from the way where the men are organized in four arrangements, Elephants, chariots, ponies, infantrymen. The Muslims of India likewise have a pack of cards that is gotten from the old images of the Tarot: the Gungeifu or Ghendgifeh.

This game is made out of eight arrangements of twelve cards.

CHINESE TAROT

An unpracticed eye may discover some trouble in perceiving the Tarot in this structure, however, the Chinese have given us a certain contention for our attestation, in the plan of their Tarot, which is spoken to by the table on page 88. We have set the correspondences of the minor what's more, major arcana, and of the four letters of the Tetragrammaton's', over the table being referred to.

A depiction of this Chinese pack will be found in Court de Gébelin {Le Monde Primitif) and in the work of J. A. Vaillant. With respect to other European Tarots, we have duplicates of almost all and this instigates us to name the different releases which we have been empowered to counsel.

THE FRENCH TAROT PACKS

The Tarot of Etteila is of no emblematic worth; it is a terrible mutilation of the genuine Tarot. This pack is utilized by afflicting our crystal gazers. Its sole intrigue lies in the abnormality of its figures. It very well may be acquired for 5 or 8 francs from distress the extraordinary card-dealers in Paris.

The Tarot of Watillaux, or pack of the Princess Tarot recreates the minor arcana accurately. It is worth thought on this record. The Italian Tarot, that of Besancon and of Marseilles, are undeniably the best which we have, especially the last, which decently recreates the crude symbolical Tarot.

THE GERMAN TAROT

Other than the Italian, we should make reference to the German Tarot, in which the images of the minor arcana are extraordinary. The Cups are spoken to by The Hearts, The Pentacles, The Bells, The Swords „ The Leaves The Scepters, The

Acorns, Be that as it may, this Tarot is an awful one.

THE TAROT OF OSWALD WIRTH

It got important to have a Tarot pack in which the imagery was unquestionably settled. This work, proposed by Eliphas Levi, who characterized the standards on which it was to be based, has been practiced by Mr. Oswald Wirth.

This sharp medium, helped by the counsel of Stanislas de Gnaita, has planned the arrangement of the twenty-two major arcana. These drawings replicate the Tarot of Marseilles, with the symbolical alterations recommended by the inquiry of Eliphas Levi upon this significant question. Having to the thoughtfulness of M. Poirel, who helped the work by printing these structures, Ave now has a radiant representative archive in the Tarot of Oswald Wirth.

It is in this manner shrewd, as Ave has just started, for the individuals who wish to contemplate the Tarot altogether, to get the Tarot of Marseilles and that of Oswald Wirth. We will utilize them both to introduce in our clarification of the symbolical significance of each card. Be that as it may, before going to the investigation of these images, card via card, Ave must check whether there is no way to emphatically characterize the imagery of the Tarot.

HOW Might WE HOPE TO DEFINE THE SYMBOLISM OF THE TAROT CONCLUSIVELY?

We have as of now and adequately clarified that the Tarot speaks to the antiquated or mysterious science in each conceivable advancement. In the event that Ave, at that point wishes to locate a strong reason for the investigation of the images spoke to! In the 22 significant arcana, we may put the Tarot on one side for a moment, and commit ourselves to this old science.

Only it can empower us to achieve our end, not in finding the clarification of the images, yet in driving us to make them individually, reasoning them from fixed and general standards. We will hence begin work of a serious new character while maintaining a strategic distance from, so far as could reasonably be expected, having into those blunders which emerge from the push to clarify the images of the Tarot without anyone else, rather than looking for their answer at their unique source.

The initial phase in the quest for these specific images leads us to talk about the grave issue of the starting point of imagery itself. We can't enter upon, considerably less unravel, this inquiry without anyone else's input; we will, in this way, quote the assessments of a few journalists upon the subject. Truth having Solidarity for its standard, the understanding of different ends. At a certain point will be a significant guide for us.

Louis Claude de Saint-Martin, the obscure scholar, States in his book, the Tableau Naturel des Affinities that the crude letter set is made out of sixteen signs. He got this information, so far as we can pass judgment, from natural disclosure, joined to the educating of a mystery school, of which he was one of the individuals. Lacour, in his book on the Elohim or Gods of Moses, has inductively decided the presence of a crude letter in order, additionally made out of sixteen signs.

Another creator, Barrois, seeking after the request of a serious extraordinary nature additionally arrives at the finish of the presence of sixteen crude signs in his System of Dactylology. But the works of Court de Gébelin, or more all of Fabre d'Olivet, are the most surprising in this regard. In his Langue Hébraïque Restituée, the last-mentioned learned Initiate set up the presence of crude hieroglyphic signs from which the Hebrew letters are determined.

Every one of these essayists, beginning from altogether different focuses, concur with their decisions, and this gives us a solid contention for the reality of their investigation. In any case, it makes a difference to know whether these 16 crude signs are the immediate birthplace, both of the Hebrew, Sanskrit, Chinese, or Greek letters. The character of the source tends emphatically to the personality of results, what's more, anybody of these subsidiary letter sets will reply to our motivation.

The Hebrew letter set, made out of 22 letters, appears desirable over us, by virtue of the concordance between the quantity of its letters and that of the Arcana in our Tarot.

We will, subsequently, receive, as the beginning stage of our examination, the Hebrew letters in order of 22 letters, inferred from the 16 crude hieroglyphic signs. This end is hardly arrived at when crisp light sparkles upon us from all sides. William Postel [1] uncovers to us the association between the Hebrew letters and the Tarot; Van Helmont the Younger, [2] L. C. de Saint-Martin, [3] Fabre d'Olivet, [4] upset affirm our feeling; finally, Éliphas

Levi 6 likewise tosses the heaviness of his superb learning into the inquiry.

Yet, we will be progressively astonished to discover that the Sepher Yetzirah, 1 an old book of the Kabalah, which contains an examination upon the development of the Hebrew letter set.

Chapter 8: Swords

The Swords suit depicts intellect and thought. These cards directly imply that you are true and just and always trust your morals.

Ace of swords- the upright ace of swords card signifies that you have a lot of clarity in terms of your thinking. You come in with a lot of power and are capable of achieving anything that you put your mind to. But you don't have a clear direction in terms of how best your powers can be used. Basically, it means that you have had enlightenment and are fully equipped to finish something that you have always wanted to finish. You have all the power to go after the truth and make sure you use it to your advantage. The reversed ace of swords card signifies that you have no clarity in terms of what you aspire to become. You have no predefined goals to follow and are lost. It will also indicate that you have a few good ideas in mind but have yet to implement them and reap their benefits. This might be because you don't have the right means to put the ideas into action and are waiting for it to come through.

Two of swords- the upright two of swords card signifies that you are confused in life and unable to come to a decision. The card showcases a blind folded woman, which means that she is oblivious to the world. This is one of those cards that give a similar reading whether it is upright or reversed. Basically, you are in a position where there is a lot of confusion and a lack of clarity. You are afraid of the consequences and are ignoring whatever difficulties are coming your way. You are in a state of denial and have reached stalemate. The reversed card gives a similar reading. The reversed two of swords card indicates that you are extremely confused and have no idea on the way forward. You might have a lot of information available with you but are unable to make sense of it. You stand on the threshold of making an important decision and are yet to move forward. It may also indicate that all is not well amongst your family members and in a bid to unite the two grieving parties; you are being made the target of their ire.

Three of swords- the upright three of swords card indicates that you have gone through a very painful rejection or are on the verge of it. It indicates that you are having a tough time in your personal life where someone has broken your heart after being with you for a very long time. The very image on the card is enough to tell you of your fate. It showcases a red heart placed in the center of a thunderstorm and three swords piercing it from top. You are grieving owing to your painful separation from your beloved. The reversed three of swords card, however, signifies that you are recovering from a broken heart. You are slowing releasing all the pain that you once felt and are in a position to forgive and forget. You are optimistic about the future and are in a good position to move forward. It is also a warning sign to those in a shaky relationship to start mending theirs or suffer from a painful heartbreak. If your relationship is strained then you need to mend it at the earliest and forgive your partner.

Four of swords-the upright four of swords card indicates that the person is recovering from something. He or she is now taking some time off to rest and recuperate before going back into the world. The card showcases a knight resting under three swords with one lying next to him. This indicates that the person has just dealt with a crisis and is taking time to recover from it. It might be a divorce or a break up or some loss such as financial or emotional. If you are still worrying about it unnecessarily, then it is high time that you took a break and calmed yourself down. The reversed four of swords indicates that you quite restless and instead of relaxing, you are forging ahead. This means that you are in no position to listen to your body's need for rest and relaxation and are completely, and unnecessarily, stressing yourself out. You have probably reached breaking point and are completely frustrated with your life's retarded growth and progress. To try and fix this situation, you are working your mind and body overtime.

Five of swords- the upright five of swords card signifies that the person is under a lot of conflict and is not in good terms with others. You have probably fought a fierce battle and won it too, but in the process you made just so many enemies that you are now completely isolated and aloof from the rest of the world. However, if you suspect that you will need to go into battle soon, and then you must prepare yourself to win instead of giving into other people's whims and fancies. The card showcases a person wielding a couple of swords with two others walking away. The reversed five of swords indicate that the person is open to truce and in a position to befriend others. It will also mean that you have run away from a conflict and decided to leave it unresolved. You might have lost that person's loyalty forever and might not have a chance to speak or interact with them again. However, you need not worry as many others will walk into your life and you don't have to sweat it over a few lost friendships.

Six of swords- The upright six of swords card indicate that the person is making a vital decision, but one that will leave them broken hearted. However, it might be extremely important to make the decision for the better good of everyone. You might feel sad temporarily but will enjoy absolute clarity once this sad phase is over. You will take solace in the fact that you are heading towards a brighter tomorrow and the decision you made is working to your advantage. It basically means that you are now completely down and depressed and not feeling good about what life is throwing at you. But you have not lost hope and are optimistic that tomorrow will be a better day. The card showcases a fully cloaked woman sitting in a boat with her head down while a man rows the boat. The reversed six of swords card signifies that you are determined to move on from a bad episode and get your life back on track. But it is not an easy road to take. You are faced with a lot of hurdles and in no position to have a smooth run. The reversed card can also indicate that you are not taking the vital decision that you need to in order to better your life. You are resisting the change instead of allowing it to help you better your life. If you have just entered a new relationship then the reversed card indicates that you are in no position to move on and forget about a past relationship.

Seven of swords- the upright seven of swords card indicates that you are trying to stealthily run away from something that you have done and has caused others loss. It means that you are looking for ways to go unnoticed after having betrayed someone or causing them harm. It will also mean that you are trying to slowly run away from a relationship just because it is not intriguing you anymore. You are not directly telling the other person that it is over and are instead sneakily moving away. Again, it might also indicate that you need to be careful as someone might be trying to do that with you. So try and remain as mindful and cautious as possible and don't let anyone hurt you. The card showcases a man carrying swords and trying to run away while looking backwards. The reversed seven of swords card indicates that you are struggling to move in a different direction. You are holding to your past, which is causing you to not make positive progress. This is the primary card that showcases you are having an extra marital affair and are living on the edge. The arrival of this reversed card indicates that it is best you decide to open up to your partner about the affair instead of putting on a charade and keeping him or her in the dark.

Eight of swords-the upright eight of swords card is an indication that you are punishing yourself for something that you have done. You might have a certain set of ideals and are assuming that you are incapable of living up to them. You feel trapped inside your thoughts and feelings. You are not able to think beyond a certain limit and are completely bound on all sides with your own limited thoughts and ideals. This is making you make all the wrong decisions and so, it is best to lie low now and not make any new ones. The card showcases a blindfolded woman standing in the center of a piece of land surrounded by puddles and there are 8 swords all around her. The reversed eight of swords card signifies that you are now ready to accept something and move past it. Even if you have been betrayed, you are not feeling worried and have decided to move past it. You prefer not to be the victim and are determined to prove to your betrayer that you are ready to move past it.

Nine of swords-the upright nine of swords card indicates that you have probably hit the lowest point mentally and are suffering from extreme depression and nightmares. You have a lot of anxiety and are in no position to think straight. It is probably the worst phase of your life. The card is said to be the most dreaded in tarot and has an extremely negative vibe about it. The card showcases a person sitting on the bed and covering face with palms with nine swords hanging on the wall next to him. You can sense the pain that the person in the card is feeling and how he is unable to sleep at night due to the worry. The reversed nine of swords card indicates that the person is driving themselves mad owing to the anxiety and depression but in reality, it is not necessary to stress out so much. The bad phase will pass for sure and you will have a better life to look forward to. The card can also signify your journey towards a better tomorrow and have worked through your bad phase. You are finally getting to sleep without worry and it is best that you pay attention to your dreams and interpret them to help you make positive progress.

Ten of swords- the upright ten of swords card indicates that you are in trouble. You are going to have a sudden loss and it might be because of someone taking advantage of you. You will be backstabbed and mercilessly abandoned by your betrayer or betrayers. There will be no warning signs and you will have to deal with the consequences of betrayal and feel anguished by it. Since there were no signs of an upcoming betrayal, you were not at all prepared for one and thus, have been defeated and a crisis has been brought upon you. The card showcases a man lying face down on the ground and ten long swords piercing his back. The reversed ten of swords card indicates that something has to end in order for something new to start. This new phase will bring in a lot of good luck and so it is best to put an end to past endeavors, even if it means killing it. The reversed card might also mean that you are not open to moving past something that is pulling you down or you are still delving in a past bad experience and allowing it to affect your current life. The wounds are still fresh and you are hurting beyond reason.

Page of swords-the upright page of swords card indicates that you are full of energy and enthusiasm. You are extremely passionate and start all your endeavors with a lot of excitement. In fact, you are ready to go on an adventure and the arrival of this card indicates that it is ideal for you to start on it without further ado. You have all our plans and ideas sorted out and it is only a matter of time before you put your ideas into action. You are curious to get started and can't wait to go ahead. The card showcases a young man with long open hair standing confidently by the sea and wielding a sword high in the air. You can sense the passion, curiosity and enthusiasm that he has in him. He also looks like a very talkative person and so are you. The reversed card, however, indicates that you are all talk and don't put any of it into action. You will make big plans for yourself but not pursue any of them. You might also promise to others many things but not act on them. So it is best to not do so and be careful of what you tell others.

Knight of swords-the upright knight of swords card indicates that you are ready to jump into something and are determined to achieve it. You are not thinking it through and are forging ahead with an idea. You are just so obsessed with it that you are ready to move forward without even having a plan of action. You have come into a lot of energy and are determined to begin work at the earliest. And once you decide to start, there is just no stopping you. This card signals that you are sure to start on something new at the earliest and are determined to finish it. You are not thinking of the consequences but are communicating your idea well enough and others are helping you in the process. The card showcases a knight riding his horse and raising the sword high in the air. You can feel the passion and enthusiasm that he has. The reversed knight of swords card indicates that you are extremely impatient and in no mood to stop and listen to others, even if they are giving you good advice. But this need not mean a bad thing. Ding your own thing and making mistakes will only benefit you. You will have a chance to learn from your mistakes and not taking advice from others will help you remain self sufficient and happy.

Queen of swords-the upright queen of swords card indicates that you are extremely organized and a very quick thinker. You have the capacity to think things through and come up with a feasible decision. You don't have to put in a lot of effort for it and it comes to you naturally. You are stern and mature and have seen the ways of the world. If you have received this card and are not like that then it is an indication that you need to be independent and mature in taking your decisions. You should not bother or care for others' feelings and tell something like it is. The card showcases the queen sitting on the throne with a sword in her hand and the other hand gesturing to "rise". The reversed queen of swords card indicates that you are extremely emotional and your feelings are quite unstable. They keep swinging and there are times when you indulge in bitching about others around you. You are not at all bothered about others' emotions and don't think twice before saying something nasty about them. In fact, indulging in these activities is causing you to waste your time and you are better off doing productive things in life.

King of swords-the upright king of swords card indicates that you are someone with a lot of authority. The upright kings are always a good sign and this one is no different. You will think clearly and are capable of making fair decisions. Once you make the decision you are stern about it and don't encourage anybody to question it. You can be opinionated and most of the time, others laud your opinions. You might have a lot of control over others and they come up to you to seek advice. You are capable of looking at something through all possible angles and then come up with a feasible decision that pleases both parties. Apart from helping others, you make use of your intelligence to progress in life. Another thing that this card indicates is that you might need some good advice yourself. This can be in regard to your personal or financial life and you have to ask for the right advice for you to make positive progress. The card showcases a king sitting on his throne with a sword in his hand. He commands authority and respect. The reversed king of swords card signifies that you are extremely manipulative and will have it your way no matter what the consequences. You will persuade others to listen to you and get them on board even if it is the wrong choice for them. You will also not have clarity and be in a bad position to choose what is best for you. Your thinking is extremely scattered and not at all precise.

Chapter 9: Tarot Cards Reading And Psychic Reading

If you're having trouble using your intuition, you can go a step further to see what your psychic choice would be. It might seem counter-intuitive that making a psychic choice would be more comfortable than making an intuitive choice, but the trick in this instance is your eyes. When you're working through intuition, you'll want to keep your eyes open so that you're using some part of your mind to make the selection. It's crucial that you struggle through what's logical versus what's deeper, more genuine, and emotional.

When you're working through psychic potential, however, you'll want those eyes 100% shut. Close off your physical body to any influences whatsoever, and let your psychic powers guide your choice. Again, this method works for both in-store and online shopping. For online shoppers, gather all the potential items in your "shopping cart," close your eyes, spin around a few times if you can, and then point out the deck that's meant to be yours. Open your eyes at the very end to see which one you selected.

Tarot Tools

There are many places that you can go to when looking for any of the tools. In this era of technology, the first place I'd recommend would be the internet. Keep in mind, however, that doing your shopping this way can be quite tricky.

Spreads

You can always just draw one card. And then after a while, when your understanding of the cards has increased, look up some three-card spreads on the internet, you can use the one mentioned in the guide book you're using, or you might just want to do it intuitively.

Candles, incense, and essences

In general, aromatherapy is prevalent for the people belonging to this community. Essences can heal your moods and your physical aches, and hence, can make you feel more at home and safe in your sacred place. Typically, these tools like the candles can be found in the same place where you got your tarot cards. Not that finding natural essences is difficult but finding a deck might just be a little hard, so there you have a tip.

Crystals or gemstones

Another thing that might help with the tuning-into and with feeling safe and relaxed is using crystals. There is really nothing else to explain for this term. I really do mean minerals made in the earth, like Rose Quartz, Lapis Lazuli, and Tiger's Eye. The chemical structure found in these minerals is said to invest them with a sort of memory, and that is what is used.

People push their emotions and intentions into the crystal, and 'program' it. Once that is done, the crystal will remember it and radiate that emotion or intention into the environment. You'll see then how you could use crystals to make a room feel a certain way.

A Silk Scarf

All physical objects collect 'impressions' or 'vibrations' from their surroundings and Tarot cards are no exception. Some people are able to 'read' these impressions, and give an accurate rendering of past events from inanimate objects, but while this is interesting, it is not always desirable.

Silk is a fabric that for some reason rejects such 'impressions', and the purpose of the scarf is to keep your cards clean of 'vibrations' that might otherwise adversely affect the quality or accuracy of your readings and meditations. As it is a tradition in the occult that all tools should be hand-made, it would be a good idea to buy some silk (a piece about a foot square will do nicely) and make the scarf yourself.

A Wooden Box

When the cards have been wrapped in silk, they should be kept in a wooden box. This box serves the same purpose as the scarf, and wood is chosen as the material for much the same reasons as silk is the preferred substance for the scarf. It further protects the cards from adverse 'vibrations' and at the same time preserves them from prying eyes and fingers, and physical wear and tear or accident - spilled coffee for instance, or water from a vase overturned by the family cat.

A Tarot Cloth

The Tarot cloth is another piece of silk, usually a yard or more square, and fringed.

It is used to cover the surface on which you intend to lay out the cards for meditation or reading, and as it is of little use to wrap and box the cards and then lay them out on a surface that may be sticky as well as generally unsuitable, you should make an effort to own one.

How to read the cards?

When you have collected together all of the above items, you will be ready to start 'breaking in' your Deck - for a Tarot Deck has to be 'broken in' just like a new pair of shoes. For the first month or so after getting your Deck, you should carry it with you everywhere (sans box of course) and sleep with it under your pillow. You should also handle it as much as you possibly can. This will serve to 'activate' you to your Deck, and vice versa; and if you are new to the Tarot, it will help you become accustomed to and familiar with the design and feel of your cards.

Never let anyone else handle your Deck. It is very personal to you despite the fact that many thousands of people own one just like it. If your friends want to handle and examine Tarot cards (and they will, if they see you handling and examining yours!) then they must buy a Deck of their own. You must not allow them to satisfy their curiosity with your Deck, as this will undo all the work of 'activation' you have begun, and totally negate the protective qualities of your scarf and box.

Choose the deck you want to use. It is important to note that different decks would use different symbolism. As mentioned in the previous chapter, the most commonly used would be the Rider-Waite tarot or one of its other versions such as the Morgan-Greer tarot. Professionals would tell you to let the tarot speak to you instead. It's all in the feeling you get from the deck itself.

Slowly begin transferring some of your energy onto the deck. To do this, one must simply handle the cards. Shuffle them, arrange them in order and simply familiarize yourself with it. In due time, these cards can become an extension of you as well.

The major arcana. These would represent the different stages we go through in life. It is meant to be a picture story of the journey itself, starting from the fool (which is young energy in spirit form) and moves on through the different events that happen and ends in finding completion within the world.

The minor arcana. These cards are representative of people, feelings, events as well as circumstances that we might encounter during the journey. It represents the events which are within our control and also indicates how you should go about doing something. The minor arcana is similar in looks to your traditional playing card deck.

Get a good book to guide you but don't rely heavily upon it. Learn the basics from it but when it comes to tarot reading, your instincts would always be best. Let that guide you instead. There's no need to worry about being right and simply work with what your gut is telling you. Memorizing is one thing but beyond that, it's about connecting with your cards and letting them speak to you.

It is essential that everything happens naturally, avoid forcing the cards to give you answers because then it might produce inaccurate results. As a reader, you should also remember that in some way, you do influence the cards. So if you're energy is running afoul and you might not be in the best of moods, this could manifest itself as well. It is because of this reason that many people meditate before doing a reading. This is to help calm their nerves as well as clear their head.

Get to know the deck a bit more.

Choose any random card and study it for a bit, make a note of your first impression of it as well as any intuitive thoughts. Do this repeatedly for each card, write comments and any other observation that you infer from it. Do you get a positive feeling from it? A negative one? What made you feel this way? These are just some of the questions you can ask.

Find a quiet place. If you like you can also light a candle, incense, and put on some soft, soothing, meditation music at low volume in the background.

Place your Deck of the 22 Major Arcana Tarot Cards in front of you. Begin breathing in, slowly and deeply, then exhaling slowly.

Continue to breath slowly and deeply, in and out, for several minutes. Close your eyes. Imagine yourself being bathed in a beautiful white light. See yourself glowing. See your entire aura flooded with this beautiful, brilliant white light.

Continue to breath slowly, in and out. Visualize a beautiful rose-colored light glowing in your heart area. As you continue to breathe slowly, see this rose-colored light grow larger and larger and larger.

And after a few minutes, inwardly ask a question. Make the question a specific one. The more specific the question, the better result you will obtain.

And then pick up your cards, and begin to shuffle them over and over while silently asking your question. Keep shuffling until you feel that it is the correct time to stop.

This is something that you will just feel. You cannot make a mistake.

Then, place the cards on the table in front of you. Cut the deck into 3 piles with your left hand. Put the deck back together in whatever way you feel led to do.

Next, place the 4 top cards, face down, in a row, on the table in front of you. Put the rest of the deck aside. Now, turn over the first card.

The first card will give you information about the past, as it relates to your question. If the card is upside down, just turn it right side up and begin gazing at it softly.

Please feel free to refer to this book while doing so if necessary to interpret the card. I do suggest that you try first to let it just speak to you by gazing at it before looking at the meaning in the book. You may be surprised that you receive some additional insight this way.

Next, turn over the 2nd card. This card represents the present, as it relates to your question. Again, gaze softly at it for a few minutes before looking at your book for help.

If something pops into your mind, then pay attention to it.

Next, turn over the 3rd card. This card represents the future as it pertains to your question. Gaze at it softly and allow it to reveal its message to you.

Lastly, turn over the fourth card. This card represents the best that can be hoped for in the situation pertaining to your question.

Did you find that any information was revealed to you? Did anything usual happen to you during the reading. Did your mind fill with images, or words or colors? Did you hear a voice or some words being spoken?

Practice makes perfect. Try this exercise again when you feel rested and ready. And try it with friends. See if you can get any information for them. Sometimes it is easier to read for somebody else, rather than for yourself. especially when first trying to learn to read Tarot.

And then, as always, take a few moments to quietly go inward and give "Thanks" for the information that you have received.

Here's a great tip for learning to read the Tarot. After you have experienced your first few practice readings, and have had a chance to "feel" what that is like, you may want to try using a tape recorder or app on your phone or tablet.

In this case you would speak your reading out loud into the recording device. When you start speaking in this way, many times you will find yourself just saying some things spontaneously that really shed more light on your reading.

To make the best use of every tarot card reading, it is best to adopt a positive attitude and follow specific guidelines.

Reverse Cards

One thing I would point out on the subject is that reversal of the cards doesn't mean that the meaning of the card is reversed in its entirety either. Often, the reversal of a card simply means that the energy or intensity of the action in the reversed card is at the opposite end of that in the upright card.

So, for example, Death does not mean perishing physically, but instead signifies a time of change, big or small. The change may be ideological, inspirational, or the death of a previously cherished system of thought—which shall then lead to newer opportunities and ideologies. It's essential to remember that no meaning or interpretation within the Tarot is finalistic, but they are all cyclical.

So, if one door closes, another will open. Either way, in case of reversed Death, reversal means that change is still coming, but its intensity is far less than that signified by the upright card. This system usually applies to all reversals, with the only change between upright and reversed being the magnitude of the effect.

Practice Exercises for reading the cards

Before moving on to learning the meanings of cards and different types of spreads, let us establish a clear understanding of the two different kinds of readings and attitude you need to adopt before every reading to make the most of it.

Keep Your Mind and Options Open: Do not begin with an answer already set in your mind; instead, keep a more open approach to the reading and ask a question with different possibilities.

Focus on a Problem Broadly: When you ponder on a specific issue or a question in particular, do not just fixate on one or two details and aspects only. Instead, adopt a more open approach to it and at it broadly.

Clear Your Head: When focusing on a problem, clear your head first by taking a few deep breaths. Count up to 5 when inhaling through your nose, hold the breath for another count of 5 and then release it through your mouth to a count of 7. Take 5 to 10 deep breaths using this technique and focus on your breathing alone. You will feel a lot calmer than before and will find it easier to concentrate on the problem at hand and nothing else.

Be Specific: While you should focus on a problem broadly, you need to be specific about the query or aspect of life you wish to reflect on and get more insight about in the tarot reading. You cannot focus on 10 different aspects and expect to resolve them all at once through one reading.

Pay Attention to Yourself: If the issue is relevant to you, focus on yourself and ask a question about yourself. You need to be the center of the reading and nobody else. For instance, if you are concerned about where your relationship with your current partner is going, do not ask if he/she loves you, but focus on what the relationship means to you and whether you see a future with that person.

Learn to Read between the Lines: Reading between the lines is one skill you need to learn when reading tarot cards. Analyze every card in its literal and then figurative aspects and see if there is a hidden message in every word.

Accept the Reading: Whether you are having an automated reading with tarot cards online or carrying out a session manually yourself and reading real cards, you may be tempted to conduct another reading instantly if the first one did not give you the answers you were looking for.

Be Optimistic: Adopt a very positive attitude towards the reading and instead of focusing on why something has not happened or how an event negatively affects you, focus more on how things can be improved.

Be Neutral: Make sure that your questions do not convey preconceived notions making you feel that your viewpoint is the only correct option. For example, focusing on why you are earning more money than your partner earns and contributing to the finances is not neutral; but thinking of ways to get him/her to cooperate more in the financial matters is a more neutral approach to tackling the problem.

Significators

When you are giving a Tarot reading, you will need to sue a spread from the cards that are in the tarot deck. There are a lot of spreads that you could choose from. These spreads always provide a different meaning for every reader and can be used for specific readings. These spreads could involve picking up all the cards in the deck or even two cards! The spread that is used most often is the Celtic cross spread.

When you are about to begin a reading, you could select a card from random on the deck, which would work as a representation for the person who is receiving his or her reading. This card is called the Significator. The Significator is a card that has its own position in most spreads, including the Celtic cross spread. There are other spreads for which it can be drawn from the deck right before the reading.

The reason behind choosing the significator card helps the reader, which you to focus better on the seeker is. This chosen card could be used to depict a characteristic of the seeker or any other personality traits that are hidden. This card is sometimes chosen to represent an issue that is relevant to the subject under consideration.

The Significator is chosen by the reader and is used to signify the characteristic of the person who was receiving the reading. This is not always drawn by the reader, but could be depending on the spread or the reader. The court cards are always good to use as the representation of human nature and character. This is because these cards are all symbolically and pictorially human.

The best example of this is the Queen of Cups. The queen consists of a mystery, which is feminine and also talks about fragility and keen intuition. A person who has the following characteristics would have great power of seduction, which does not necessarily have to be associated with beauty.

This person would know how to gain attention without demanding it. The Queen of Cups is often hurt easily and would need protection. However, it is not necessary that only a court card needs to be used to depict the nature of a person. You could also use any other card from the deck!

This is true with respect to many aspects of the Tarot. There is no rule that needs to be followed strictly when you are choosing the Significator for a tarot reading. The reader has the right to decide whether or not to incorporate the Significator in the reading. If the Tarot reader has decided to use a spread, which has the Significator in it, the reader can always choose to ignore the position if they do not wish to use the Significator during their reading.

But, if they do they will need to incorporate the Significator and also select the card before the reading.

There are multiple ways by which the Significator could be selected. This includes matching the characteristics of the human being with the card in hand. You could also choose a card at random if you prefer. It all depends on you when it comes to selecting the Significator.

How to use Intuition to read cards?

When it comes to matters such as reading tarot cards or other forms of intuitive or psychic, divination, you often hear someone's ability to communicate in this way as a gift. You can go ahead and think of it as a gift if you want to, as long as you acknowledge that it is one that we are all born with.

The ability to attune oneself with the inner voice, or intuition, is one that resides in all of us. It is quite simply a matter of being open to it and learning to recognize when it speaks.

Unfortunately, most of us are so disconnected from our intuitive voice that we no longer recognize it. Have you ever just had a feeling about something, or thought about something quite randomly, only to have it show up later in the day? These are just a couple of examples of the many ways your intuitive voice speaks to you every day.

Reading tarot cards don't require a gift of any type, except for the gift you give yourself of learning how to connect with your inner voice.

Intuition goes by many names.

You might have heard it referred to as psychic ability, spiritual enlightenment, higher self, higher consciousness, or universal energy. These are all names for the same thing; simply being attuned to messages from the universe. Each one of us is a part of the universal energy. Everything is connected. Every thought you have, every action you take or don't take, causes a ripple that expands out through the entire universe.

This is a large concept to grasp at first, and might even seem to highly improbable. Think about the last time you had a bad day and the random people that you may have been a little. It is possible that they were going through their own inner turmoil and your interaction was just enough to send them over the edge.

They, in turn, spread more negativity and on it goes. The same applies to spread positivity and compassion. The smallest acts have significant impact. This is because we are all connected by a web of vibrational energy.

Knowing that this energy exists is one thing, but acknowledging how this energy is manifested within each of us is something entirely different. Tarot has been, and in some circles still is, associated with dark magic.

The idea has prevailed over the years that if you have developed the intuitive ability to read and translate an illustrated deck of cards that you are somehow connected to negative energy and dark worship. While, there are certainly people who use the tarot for dark purposes, this does not represent the overwhelming majority of tarot readers.

Reading tarot cards and developing your spiritual powers is all about tapping into this energy. You must be open to it. The energy and vibrations are there, but they will not travel through a sealed-off entrance. Most of us start off being very open to this energy, but because of the way we live today, by the time we reach adulthood we are far removed from the original place of innocence and receptiveness of our early years.

Those that seem to have a "gift", simply could maintain an openness rather than closing themselves off.

To connect with your intuition on the level that is required to read tarot cards, you must begin opening that pathway and breaking down the walls built up in the entranceway. This is not a complicated process, but it does require a little effort, patience and introspection. It is the introspection aspect that some people have a difficult time with. Trust me that if you work through this challenge that you will be greatly rewarded.

Every time that you use your tarot cards you will find something new to learn about the cards. If you approach a professional tarot reader, he will claim that the process is never-ending. Whenever you perform a reading for yourself, you will have a different perspective about you depending on the spread that you have used. In order to understand the cards better and to trust the deck of cards, you will need to handle the tarot cards that you own with utmost care.

You could either try the single card or the three-card spread and practice. If you are a beginner, it is best to use the three-card spread, which is explained in detail in the next chapter. You can worry more about the cards a little later.

It has been seen over time that there are a few cards, which would begin to hold a specific meaning to you. In spite of that you will find that you receive these flashes of intuition when you hold a card in front of you. These flashes would leave you with a meaning that you would have never thought of before. This is why it is always good to choose your very own deck of cards and try to maintain a personal relationship with them. This would help you develop your very own interpretations of your cards!

When you have chosen a deck of Tarot cards that you know you would love, you will have to understand these cards better.

Put the booklet that has come with the cards away and start taking a good look at the cards that are in the deck. You could start with the Fool card. This is the first card that you will find in the major Arcana. You could either do this or pick a card at random from the deck. You will have to look very closely at the card.

Look at the colors and the symbols of the card. You will also have to see what exactly the picture is depicting. You will then be able to understand your feelings and also try to interpret the meaning behind those feelings.

Try a few of these to enhance your tarot experience or to help clear mental and spiritual blockages as they arise.

Meditate. Sit quietly for just ten to fifteen minutes a day. This will relax you and make you more receptive to the vibrations of spirit energy.

Practice visualization. You can start out by visualizing something concrete and then move on to creative visualization. Pick an object, preferably one that is familiar, yet you couldn't name every detail of.

Get outside. It is difficult to connect with the energy of the universe if you are always within the confines of four walls. If you believe in fairies, sprites and nature spirits, then you know that spending just a little bit of time being observant in the outdoors opens you up to incredible experiences and observations.

Ask to be introduced to your spirit guides. Obviously, you can't physically knock on their door and introduce yourself. Meeting your spirit guides require meditating on the subject and being receptive to the subtlest of clues. Begin by asking a name. You might not hear the name spoken, but I bet a name instantly pops into your head. Go with it. This is an example of your intuitive voice.

Write your own book of tarot meanings. Grab a journal and don't read the following chapters of this book until you have created a book that tells your tarot story and what the cards mean to you.

Connect with something old. One of my favorite ways of developing my energies is to visit an antique store, a museum or a really old house. If you can, touch a few things and pay attention to what you are feeling. Do any images or thoughts pop into your mind. If so, you could be picking up on the energy that an object has been carrying around with it for years.

Stay as healthy as possible. Remember that your body is your vessel. It is the medium that your spirit guides and the universal energy travel through. If you are experiencing disharmony within your body it can be more challenging to receive and interpret these energies accurately. Practice good self-care. Get plenty of sleep, eat healthy, natural foods and tend to your emotional and mental health needs.

Chapter 10: Waite Tarot -

Information About Waite Tarot

Waite Tarot is one of the most popular existing card games. Card reading has been around for a long time. People turn to the prediction of the future to get answers to their most desired questions. In 1909, A. email. Waite created his famous cards and was issued by the rider company, thus getting the name of The Rider-Waite Tarot card. There are a lot of articles about tarot cards and reading outside, so I'll talk about the meaning of the inverted card.

Each time, when the player mixes cards, some of them end upside down; for beginners, it is recommended to ignore it and turn it in the right direction. Once the newcomer has gained experience, he should start paying attention to the inverted card. Everyone knows that each Waite Tarot card symbolizes certain energy, and when the reading of the Cards is carried out, the energy collection gives the answer to the researcher. It is commonly known that cards collect energy when mixed and cut. Energy is of a different nature; some are strong, others are weak, others stay in your life, some leaves, as the energies are distributed, you decide the exact situation.

Every time you act on a vertical card, then its energy is free to manifest itself, the characteristics, which contains the Waite Tarot card, are readily available and active, but when we deal with inverted cards, the energy is not fully developed. It can be considered that it is in the early stages or loses energy, is incomplete, or even unavailable. The features of these maps are present, but they cannot be expressed completely.

It is a good idea that you keep track of how many cards you deal vertically and how many upside down. If most Cards are straight, then your energies are free and strong. In this case, the purpose is clear. If the opposite happens, then you have little energy, and the goal is tarnished. If energies are not freely developed, they go wherever they want.

Waite Tarot Cards are a great tool for contact with the energies around us. Life is an endless flow of energy; when a person understands this flow and uses it creatively, then anything will be possible. We should not pretend that inverted cards add a different aspect of your value, and this helps you better interpret Waite Tarot cards.

Tarot Cards Spread

Tarot Cards are distributed differently depending on the questions you want to find answers to. The spread of the Celtic cross is popular because it responds to many aspects, including the current condition of the person, past events, affecting the present, and a possible future that may or may not occur. Dissemination of reports is another common spread, and it reveals the current status of her report, the way the message is controlled, and what aspects of the report should be considered.

Other spreads include astrological, Planetarium, Tetraktys, Cross and Triangle, Mandala, star guide, Tree of life, past, life, and dream spread.

For centuries, people depended on reading tarot cards and palms to predict future events. Gifted persons carried out these data for a fee. The practice is still present in today's modern world, and many people still consult the reader. The beliefs of those who go for reading vary greatly. Some believe in an unchanging fate and use the information to prepare themselves to face everything that happens to them.

Others use the information to make the right choice. These people and entrepreneurs usually occupy positions of responsibility. They want to know the consequences of their actions and the impact of their decisions on their performance. Despite the goals of physical reading, practice is gaining great popularity in society.

What tarot cards are on the market

Many types of tarot cards are available on the market. When mixed, form a pattern on the surface, such as a table. The template is tarot spreads, and each tarot reader has its favorite templates. As with many professions, when a new person begins to work, he must start with simple basic tasks. New Tarot readers should start with simple tarot cards. Deviations differ in the number of cards in the range. Simple deviations include five to one card. The rest includes between six and all cards in the tarot package.

What determines the deviations of the tarot card

The type of spread of tarot cards depends on the questions to which the client wants to answer. Some popular models are suitable for certain questions, and depending on the specific needs of the customer. Reading tarot cards is not difficult to read. The requirement of the reader is the concentration and ability to interpret the meaning of different patterns of Tarot multiplication. This requires great cognitive abilities and memorizing skills.

The simplest scatter is the scatter of three cards. The player mixes the deck, then divides it into three piles. Then the reader takes the card from each pile and puts it on the table with his face. The reader should keep the question in mind during all these activities and focus on the answer. The map on the left side of the tray presents a history question, while the map in the center is associated with the current events surrounding the question. The last card on the right represents the possible future of the problem.

Another extension of tarot cards for beginners is the spread of tarot cards with four cards. To interpret this, the reader mixes the cards with the question in mind. Then the player takes four cards from the top of the deck and spreads them on the table face down and from left to right. The first tarot card from left to right represents the past, the second present, and the third Future of the application. The fourth card is the answer to the question.

Tarot Myth Busters

The purpose of this book is to try to clarify obsolete and unnecessary superstitions related to reading Tarot cards.

Ask all experienced and ethical readers of tarot cards, if they believe that tarot cards are bad, the work of the devil, and only psychics and clairvoyants can read them, they can leave with a laugh. I would have done the same thing. The more I use and work with these cards, the more I understand their true meaning and capabilities.

When using cards with a group of people who claim to have no knowledge of tarot cards, it is always fascinating to hear the answer when the death card spins. A strong hold of breath is, to put it mildly, a whisper: "Oh, death!'. Everyone was sitting at the table, do not mislead us, that I really did not understand the death map; they were led to believe the wrong meaning for this map and more. Then what happens is that eventually, I will explain the correct meaning and convince them of this fact, with the impression that they prefer the drama of the original meaning.

Most cards are made of wood pulp and Printing Ink, created in card shapes with an image on one side and a pattern on the back, all 78 cards. Which is exactly what they are and everything they will ever be. Even digital images are just a display of the image of symbols and works of art. It is the meaning that is the most interesting part.

Tarot has evolved over the centuries, with their history perhaps starting from 15 playing cards. A century, maybe even earlier. Their development as a divination tool is not very clear, but many use a lot of elements as a tool in the future, including; throwing animal bones, chicken entrails, throwing dice, runes, consuming drugs from plants, looking into a bowl of water, plus the elegant art of drinking cup, sometimes I used cappuccino foam and I know beer is used too.

Hollywood is also responsible for many myths today; the meaning of the devil's map has been edited so that it is abused to show the real death in the film. It is a cheap supplement to add atmosphere and fear. Tarot readers are depicted as the mysterious companion, dressed in flowing clothes, with turbans, excessive jewelry, and bad taste; actors are without exception depicted as gypsy fortune-tellers in a tent or caravan with a crystal ball on the table. It's about showcases and hammers.

Superstition around the Tarot is a work of fiction, perhaps built by people who want to add mystery and control; they can fabricate an idea that they have special mastery, secret knowledge, and gifts. It is an attraction to hide their insecurity. If the tarot reader is good, he has nothing to prove, word of mouth will be enough. The wardrobe of unusual clothes is the last thing that a decent Tarot card needs to increase its reputation.

Most superstitions are quite recent, in the last century, gained momentum with the advent of cinema, television, and a significant increase in the number of people interested in Tarot. These myths also increased in volume and were heavily embroidered along the way.

We distract the most popular:

You should never buy your own tarot cards.

If that were the case, I would still be waiting for my first card game. I don't know why or where it started; it doesn't make sense. This is a very good thing, who else will know exactly what style of cards you like or "talk?" Enjoy looking at the different styles in bookstores and online, ask to see friends, maps, valuable research, and collection of different Tarot decks. In the end, you can design your own.

Never Let Others Touch Your Tarot Cards.

I understand that someone is very special and does not like all Tom, Dick, or Harry to manipulate your cards, but nothing bad will happen if others touch your deck. I've been using the same board for over 12 years, and it made me proud, when someone asks to look at their cards, they often expect me to refuse, but I'm happy to go on and explain a little bit about them. I'll stir it up. This is the perfect time to ask questions and clarify some myths.

Only fortune tellers can read tarot cards.

Yes, clairvoyants can read tarot cards, especially if they have studied them, and the same applies to everyone, we can all read them. Some people understand the cards and can read them without any exercise, but most of us will have to work. Is it possible that we all learned to read tarot cards, whether we have the right books, or/and an online course, another tarot card, which teaches us how; we all need a place to start. Enriches tarot reading, if the reader is psychic, clairvoyant and/or intuitive, there are professional readers, who do not qualify for any of the previous characteristics, but studied and practiced, until he becomes more than competent.

The purpose of this article is to try to clarify the obsolete and unnecessary superstitions associated with reading Tarot cards.

The above answer also applies to doctors, psychologists, police officers, military, and people in business, you know, they read maps. There is a package for everyone; hundreds of tarot styles, from Egyptian Arthurian, fairies, Lord of the Rings; go online and see for yourself. Outside, someone is working on their own deck of cards. There is also someone out there looking for enlightenment, advice, inner wisdom as they shuffle their tarot cards. It's for everyone. Why do witches have fun?

Tarot Cards are magical.

No, absolutely not. They are manufactured, packaged, and shipped wholesale or stored. I'm sorry if I ruined everything for you. They are used as a reading tool, symbols, meanings, and images that trigger the flow of information. Look at them as they are and avoid myths.

Tarot Cards are bad.

Tarot cards do not have magical properties or bad qualities; they are just Cards. All decent Tarot readers will use the cards to help, enlighten, show alternative options, answer questions, in a variety of good and useful ways. They would never have thought of doing it differently. Anyone who claims to use them for evil purposes is mistaken and deceives others.

We have not heard of the cards accused of wrongdoing.

The Gypsies Invented The Tarot.

There is no evidence that the Gypsies played a role in the development of tarot cards. Tarot has evolved from a deck of cards to the 15th century or earlier, in Europe, with the use of expensive, hand-painted gifts ordered by aristocrats, to serially produced woodcuts for the public to buy.

Tarot Cards Are Never Wrong.

Tarot Cards are used to illuminate the paths and options you have in your life, options, and alternatives. The future is not in the stone, but the sand, it's up to you, the future of the road you take, there may be a little more detours along the road, you will probably end up in the same place. Free will and choice to play an important role in your life and tarot cards can reflect this.

Tarot Cards Come From Egypt

These rumors and scams began with the trial of Gebelin. He misinterpreted two Egyptian words, believing that they had an average Tarot, and it was only when the rosette Stone was translated after 1799 that his error was clear.

Tarot cards cannot be read by phone

Of course, they can, it is as simple as the client asks the question, and the Tarot reader then writes the question, shuffles the cards and continues to read. This also applies to reading on the internet; this is the same technique. Just because this person, the querent, is not sitting next to you, does not mean that you cannot interact and give them answers with the help of tarot cards. Sometimes, I would type the answer and print it or email it, and it's just as valid.

Cats Will Undermine Your Skill.

When it was first suggested, my jaw took. Needless to say, I invited the four cats in the family to read that night. God knows where it started. That is not a piece of truth.

Pregnant Women Should Not Read Cards

If this were true, health warnings would be printed on the sides of card packs. It is absolutely safe for pregnant women to read the cards; they may be able to level the cards on their bump as they do.

You Can't Read Tarot Cards.

Yes, of course, you can, but first, write a question on paper and use a tarot book that you believe for answers. The trick is to use the answer books on the cards for your answer; otherwise, you can find the fight unbiased or detached. By writing all this, you can check so late.

You don't want anyone to read it, and it's a method for development.

Your tarot cards should be wrapped in silk.

Only if you like silk, I use old silk scarves that are loved and difficult to separate; this prevents the edge of the paper from scratches. In addition, it is a joy to the touch. As for my "working" platform, which lives in a gadget bag, usually purchased to protect and carry MP3 players. Two bridges and a digital recorder can fit into it. No one knows what's inside when I wear it.

Tarot Cards Are The Work Of The Devil.

Of course not. They are the work of people who want to help others, help them with the problems they have, improve their lives, discover new techniques for taking responsibility, use modern psychology. Many of these people are professional classes, doctors, psychologists, psychiatrists, nurses, scientists, consultants, etc. what circulates, happens.

The Cards Are Hidden

The word occultism means hidden. We know that the cards came from playing cards in the 15th of the XIX century, with different groups interested in them and attaching their own beliefs and meanings. The word occult has been used over the years, trying to give a false view of their true use and suggesting something wrong.

Death Map Means Death

Simply put, it means change. If you want to change careers and this map will appear in one reading, you can feel a huge sense of relief, depending on whether you know the true meaning. It's a map that filmmakers use to suggest that there will be an evil death without really appreciating what they are doing. Therefore, Tarot readers spend a lot of time reassuring their clients when this card appears. Change.

Not all tarot readers can be trusted

I can be prejudiced if I answer this! Always stick to the word when looking for someone to give you a reading. Any profession can have a charlatan, a cheater, or a woman. Just a little patience and make sure that the Tarot reader is well thought out. If you are reading and you feel very unhappy with the way things are going, make a quick exit. Ideally, you should have a feeling of well-being after reading, a feeling of clarification, do not feel like you are flying blind. Use your instincts.

Reverse Cards Are Always Terrible.

Some people choose not to use inverted cards during the game so that it sticks to 78 vertical meanings. This means you're going to lose another 78 meanings, and some of them are very, very positive. This simply means studying a little more as you learn, I suggest you look at some tarot books on online bookstores that have the best-inverted Tarot meanings. This will expand your knowledge and reading.

Conclusion

Tarot readings are still all about your soul and what you can learn from the cards, but there are many different spreads that you can try! If you can't find the one you'd like to try out in this book or online, then I recommend you try to create your own using your advanced knowledge and know-how.

www.ingramcontent.com/pod-product-compliance
Lightning Source LLC
Chambersburg PA
CBHW071455070526
44578CB00001B/347